Credits

Author: Rahat Shaukat

Illustrator: Stan Jaskiel

Pronunciation guide approved and verified by Dr. Aysha Wazwaz

Calligraphy artist: Salma Farhoune

Minor illustration work: Rahat Shaukat & Sunday Gracia.

Visit www.SprinklesOfKnowledge.com for more information about the author , upcoming projects and about the brand *Sprinkles Of Knowledge.*

Visit http://stanscartoons.com for more information about the illustrator.

Dr. Aysha Wazwaz is a seasoned Arabic teacher and also a native Arabic speaker. She has taught hundreds of kids over the years. In addition to her many other qualifications, she is an amazing human being.

Author's Note

Learning to read a new language doesn't have to be a boring and dreadful task. In fact, it can be a magical journey. Allow me to take you on one, where tales of an enchanted fair meet easy-to-follow Arabic learning.

Guiding you through Arabic letters and phonics, while saying 'hello' to new animals on every page, this book will introduce English speakers to Arabic like never before. With each letter playfully depicted as a fair attraction, with its own unique story, this is the ultimate learning experience, building association, memorizing letter shapes, and sprinkling some magic dust over study time.

I humbly hope that you and your child will have as much fun reading this book as I had creating it.

Please note: This book is intended for English speakers only. That's because this book combines Arabic phonics with English vocabulary. This book only covers Arabic letters in their isolated form. Letter transformations will be covered in a subsequent book.

Additionally, please consult audio resources for proper pronunciation. This **book is not intended to be used as** a sole resource for learning how to read Arabic.

This pronunciation guide was approved by Dr. Aysha Wazwaz, a seasoned **Arabic teacher**.

How to use this book

Umm, how do I spot the letters on a page?

Simple! Look for bright red shapes with a yellow glow around them. You can't miss them. They even have their names written under them. For example:

MEEM   WOW   YAA   ALIF

Some of the letters resemble each other. How do I tell them apart?

You can tell them apart by the number of dots on them and the position of those dots. In this book, these dots are reimagined as different objects such as wheels, glasses, ice-cream scoops, jellybeans, snoring hats, berries, cookies, and light bulbs. Also, the resembling letters are all drawn on one page, so you can compare and contrast them.

BAA   TAA   THAA   JEEM   KHAA   SHEEN   SEEN

I see that you have reimagined Arabic letters as fair attractions. How can I see what that letter actually looks like without the imagined story?

You can see the letter in simple font both as a cloud and in its text box at the bottom of the page as well.

Ok, that's great, but I don't know what these animals or words are named in Arabic. How can I figure out the sound?

You don't need to know that. In this book, Arabic letters are paired with English phonics. So, for example, if you see a rabbit with a letter, it means that letter makes the same sound as 'R.'

Ok, so I can spot a letter, but how do I know what sound it makes?

On each letter page, you will only find animals or, in a few cases, a word that starts with that letter. In some letter cases, these are the closest sounds in English. You will find letter information boxes at the bottom of the page that specifically list the sounds.

I heard that some Arabic letter sounds don't exist in English. How did you deal with those sounds?

For most of those letters, there were English sounds that were close enough to give a general idea, and they were listed to aid the reader. You should always check the information box to understand more. For the actual pronunciation of those letters, please use various audio resources.

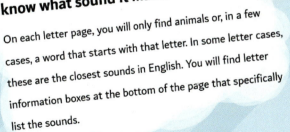

How to use this book (continued)

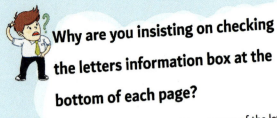

I see that some pages have more than one letter on them, so how do I differentiate which animal's name is associated with that letter?

The illustrations have some separation between each letter and the sound aiding animals around them.

Why are you insisting on checking the letters information box at the bottom of each page?

The information box is a quick summary of the letter with helpful memory jogging notes for you.

There are too many illustrations on each page for an alphabet book!

That's because this is not your typical alphabet book. It's more of a storybook that aims to make the connection between the shape of the letter and the sound it makes. So even if you don't remember the name of a letter, you will be able to remember the sound it makes and actually be able to read. In fact, don't worry about getting the names memorized. Just enjoy the story!

Ok, one last question. What is this teeth character that I see on some pages?

The wind-up teeth toy indicates that you sound that letter with the tongue placed on your teeth, as shown.

Arabic letters with names

أ ALIF

ب BAA

ت TAA

ث THAA

ج JEEM

ح HAA

خ KHAA

د DAAL

ذ DHAAL

ر RAA

ز ZAA

س SEEN

ش SHEEN

ص SAAD

ض DAAD

ط TAW

ظ DHAW

ع AIN

غ GHAIN

ف FAA

ق QAAF

ك KAF

ل LAM

م MEEM

ن NOON

ه / ٥ HAA

و WOW

ي YAA

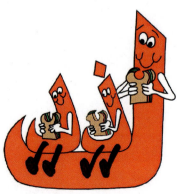

The Enchanted Fair

by

Rahat Shaukat

Illustrated by Stan Jaskiel

Scan this QR code to view the animated prequel to this book. It tells the story of how *The Enchanted Fair* came about. ->

In a town far away,

Getting ready to go.

People came from near and far,
Excited for the adventures.

They gathered at the gates, wondering what would happen next.
Then they heard beating drums and the gates swung open.

Elephants

ALIF

Alpacca

Iguana

ALIF

Letter name: ALIF.

Sounds like: A, E, I, O, and U (short U only).

ALIF for: Ant, acorn, elephant, eagle, ice cream, owl, ooh, and umbrella.

Memory jogger: A super straw letter because it is spelling most words starting with all five English vowels. Yup, you heard that right.

Let's go over here...
Wow! We are at the three canoes.
Can't tell them apart?
Their dots are the clues.

TAA's fun glasses club

Tortoise

TAA

THAA's icecream party

Three scoops of icecream

Three scoops of icecream

Three scoops of icecream

THAA

Three

Letter name: THAA.
This sound doesn't exist in English.
The closest sound is 'three' if said with the tongue positioned as shown.
Memory jogger: Three scoops party with Canoe and Three.

Letter name: TAA.
Sounds like: T.
TAA for: Turtle.
Memory jogger: Turtle and Canoe's <u>fun glasses party</u>.

BAA with his wheel, on the tightrope all day,
TAA wears glasses, so his eyes won't float away,
THAA wants to give you three scoops, if he may!

ب

BAA's balancing act

Letter name: BAA.
Sounds like: B.
BAA for: Bear.
Memory jogger: A canoe and a bear on a unicycle.

ب

Whee! The three roller coasters!
Yahoo! Like upside-down twos! But with dots! Woohoo!

HAA

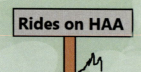
Rides on HAA

KHAA

KHAA's favorite hat party

Letter name: KHAA.
This sound doesn't exist in English.
It sounds closer to snoring.
Memory jogger: A roller coaster with a snoring hat.

Letter name: HAA.
This sound doesn't exist in English.
Sounds like: H from your throat. Like the 'haa' you would say if you ate something steaming hot.
Or the 'haa' you would say if you sighed /exhaled through your mouth, with air coming all the way back from the middle part of your throat. Or the 'haa' you would say if you fog your glasses with your mouth in order to clean them.
Memory jogger: A sighing roller coaster because he has nothing to eat.

Let's go over here now...

Duck your head from boomerang DAAL.

The wind-up teeth toy loves the dot on the DHAAL.

Boomerang zone

DHAAL

DAAL

Dog

DAAL

DHAAL

the

Letter name: DAAL.
Sounds like: D.
DAAL for: Dog.
Memory jogger: A dog throwing a boomerang.

Letter Name: DHAAL.
This sound doesn't exist in English.
The sound is 'the' if said with the tongue positioned as shown.
Memory jogger: 'The' with the dot boomerang and wind-up teeth toy.

Feel the breeze when you slide down RAA.
"I just love your dot," said the Zebra to ZAA.

RAA

ZAA

Let's go over here!
Come ride FAA,
With his bubble-making dot,
And a big round shelf to put everything you got!

Letter name: FAA.
Sounds like: F.
FAA for: Flamingo, fox, and frog.
Memory jogger: A flamingo loves the bubbles on a boat ride.

Race with **LAM**,

Fill his ladle to the brim.

Quench your thirst with yummy lemonade from him.

Letter name: LAAM.

Sounds like: L.

LAAM for: Lion, leopard, lemonade, and ladybug.

Memory jogger: A lemonade ladle.

It's NOON!
His dot spins,
Narwhal or Nina? Who do you think will win?

Can you be the last to stay on NOON's spinning dot?

Letter name: NOON.
Sounds like: N.
NOON for: Narwhal.
Memory jogger: A narwhal not falling from the dot on the pot.

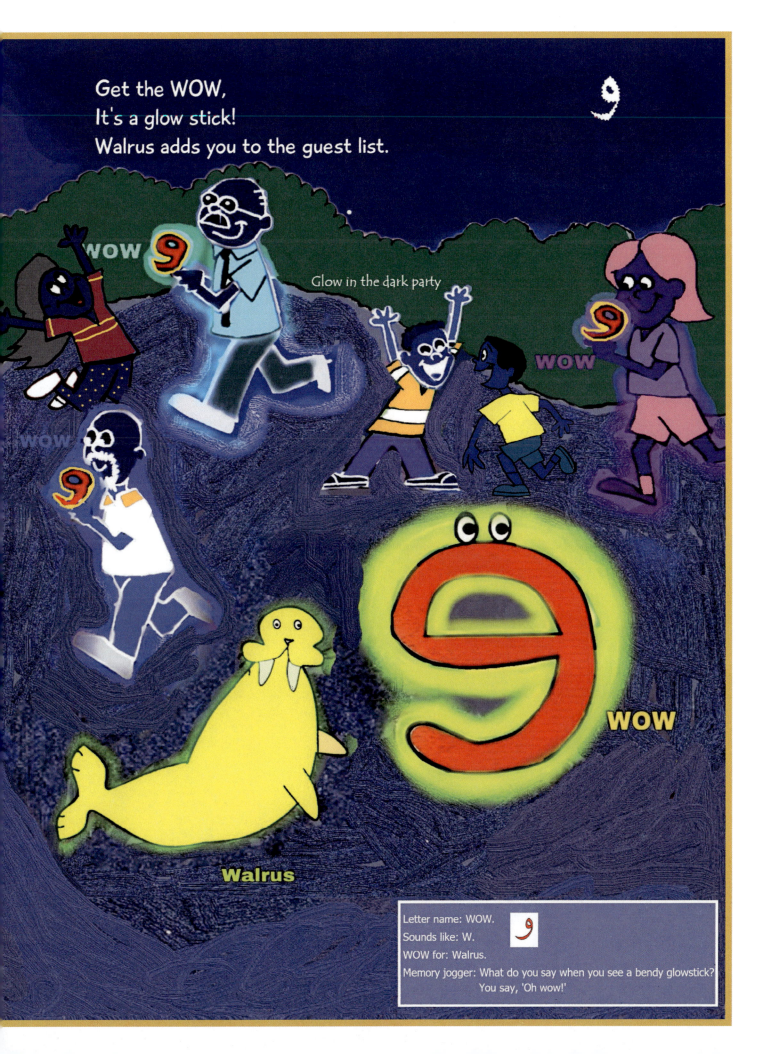

Get the WOW,
It's a glow stick!
Walrus adds you to the guest list.

Glow in the dark party

WOW

Walrus

WOW

Letter name: WOW.
Sounds like: W.
WOW for: Walrus.
Memory jogger: What do you say when you see a bendy glowstick?
You say, 'Oh wow!'

Thank you, folks! That was fun!
The fair of the Arabic letters is now done!

Pretty, shooting fireworks are one last delight.
Clap and cheer, YAY! As you enjoy the sight!

The End

Arabic Letters Tracing worksheet

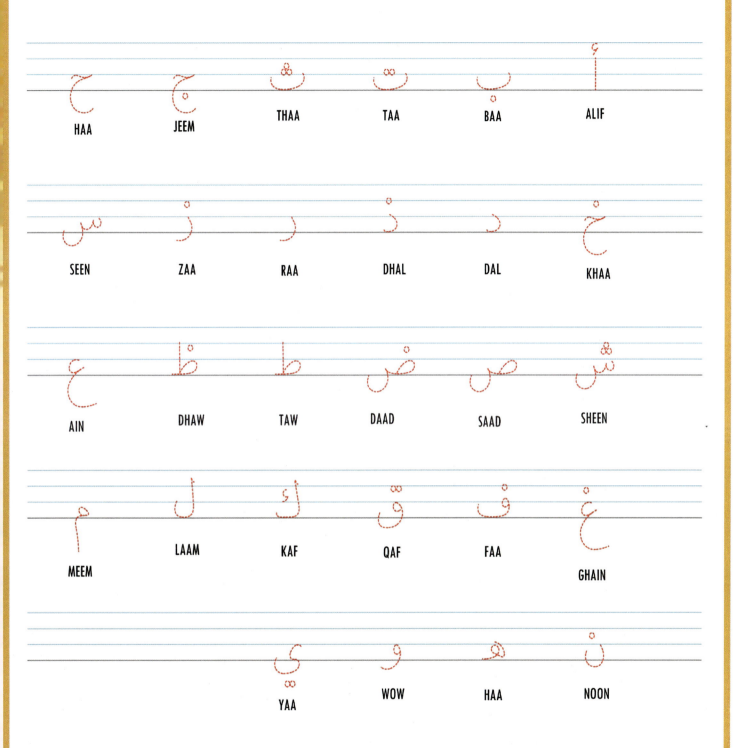

HAA	JEEM	THAA	TAA	BAA	ALIF
SEEN	ZAA	RAA	DHAL	DAL	KHAA
AIN	DHAW	TAW	DAAD	SAAD	SHEEN
MEEM	LAAM	KAF	QAF	FAA	GHAIN
	YAA	WOW	HAA	NOON	

Match the letters to the images that support their sounds.

Match the Arabic letters to the images that best support their sounds

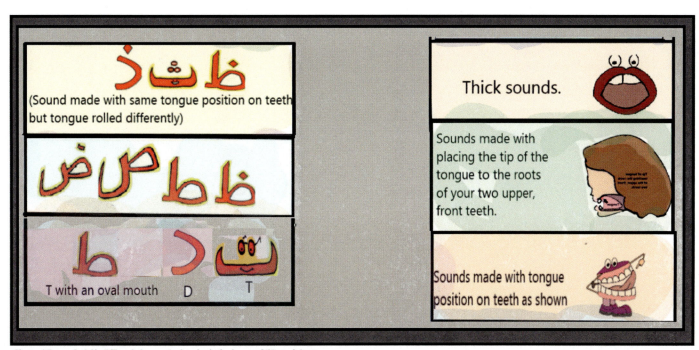

Match the Arabic letters to the images that support their sounds.

Self-quiz at the end of the book

Q1. Why was ALIF called a super letter in the book?

ALIF can spell words starting with all 5 English vowels. It makes the sound of all 5 short vowels, long A, long E, long I, and long O.

Q2. Which animal was on a unicycle, performing with the canoe letter on one wheel?

The bear. Hence the canoe on one wheel letter has the same sound as the letter 'B.'

Q3. Which animal showed up to the canoe letter with the cool glasses party?

The tortoise. Hence this letter has the same sound as the letter 'T.'

Q4. How many scoops of ice cream was the canoe letter giving out?

Three scoops.

Q5. Which two unique characters showed up to the three scoops canoe's ice cream party?

The number Three and the wind-up teeth toy. So to sound this letter, say the number three while placing your tongue on your teeth, as shown by the wind-up teeth toy.

Q6. Which animal was in line to get one free jellybean from the roller coaster letter?

The Giraffe. So the roller coaster letter with a jelly bean in his tummy makes the soft G sound or of letter J.

Q7. How was the roller coaster with no jellybean feeling?

He was hungry and hence sighing. The sighing indicates that this letter does not make a regular 'H' sound. It's a strong exhale HAA sound from the middle part of your throat.

Q8. Can you remember any of the memory cues to remember what sound the roller coaster with no jelly bean makes?

The HAA sound you make if you eat something steaming hot & spicy or if you fog your glasses to clean them, or if you let out a strong and deep sigh from the middle of your throat.

Q9. What was the hat of the third roller coaster doing?

It was snoring. So this sound doesn't exist in English, but it is close to a snoring sound. To learn the correct pronunciation, please look up an audio resource.

Q10. Which animal was throwing the boomerang letter with no dot?

The dog. Hence this letter makes the 'D' sound.

Self-quiz at the end of the book

Q11. Which two characters were hanging out with the boomerang with one dot?

The wind-up teeth toy and the word 'THE .' So to sound this letter, say the word 'THE' while placing your tongue on your teeth, as shown by the wind-up teeth toy.

Q12. Which animals/characters were hanging around to go down the slide letter with no dot?

Rabbit, rhino, raccoon, and robot. So the slide letter with no dot makes the sound of the letter 'R.'

Q13. Which animal was waiting to go down the slide letter with a dot on top?

Zebra. Hence this letter makes the same sound as the letter 'Z.'

Q14. How many cups did the food bowl letters have? How many of these cups were small, and how many were big?

Three. Two of the cups were small for ketchup and cheese. One was bigger to hold fries.

Q15. Which animal was taking orders and giving out the food bowl letter with no berries?

Skunk. Hence this letter has the same sound as that of the letter 'S.'

Q16. Which animal was taking orders for the food bowl with three shadberries?

The sheep. Shark was in line to order this bowl too. Hence this food bowl letter with three dots makes the same sound as 'SH.'

Q17. Which character was handing out milk in teacups with no cookie?

The saw. So this letter makes the thick 'S' sound that you create when you make an oval with your mouth to say the word 'saw.'

Q18. Which animal was handing out the teacup letter that came with a cookie?

The duck. So when you see a teacup letter with a dot, remember that this sound does not exist in English. It's a thick sound close to the letter D that's made with an oval mouth. See an audio source to learn the exact pronunciation.

Q19. Which animal showed up to take the ride on the merry-go-round letter with no dot on it?

Tigers. This sound does not exist in English. It's a thick sound close to the letter 'T' that's made with an oval mouth. See an audio source to learn the exact pronunciation.

Self-quiz at the end of the book

Q20. Which two characters showed up to hang out with the merry-go-round letter with a dot on it?
The oval mouth and the wind-up-teeth toy. This sound does not exist in English. It's a thick sound close to the word 'The' when said with an oval mouth and tongue positioned on your teeth as shown. See an audio resource to learn the exact pronunciation.

Q21. Which animal was riding the sky ride letter with no light bulb on it?
Aardvark. This sound does not exist in English. It's a deep strained 'A' sound when made from the middle of your throat. In fact, this letter makes all the sounds that the letter 'ALIF' makes, with the difference that the sound comes from the middle of your throat. It sounds like a strained sound. Check the letter's page for the sounds not listed here.

Q22. Which animal was sitting on the sky ride letter with a light bulb on it? What was the animal doing?
It was a goat, and it was gargling. This sound does not exist in English. The closest sound in English is the letter G if it's made while gargling. Gargling is a big clue for the sound that the sky ride letter with one dot on it makes.

Q23. Which animals were hanging around to take a boat ride on a letter with a round shelf and dot for bubble making?
Flamingo, fox, and frog. Hence this letter makes the same sound as the letter 'F.'

Q24. One of the letters had a round mouth over a big belly, and it was catching donuts in its mouth. How many eyes did the letter have?
Two. This sound doesn't exist in English. Look up an audio resource to get the exact pronunciation of this letter.

Q25. Which characters were taking a ride on the bumper car letter? Which animal was giving karate lessons on this letter as well?
Clown and coyote. Kangaroo. Hence this letter makes the same sound as that of the letter 'K.'

Q 26. Which animals were running in the race with lemonade filled in the letter shaped like a ladle?
Leopard and lion. So a ladle-shaped letter makes the same sound as the letter 'L.'

Q27. Which animal was sitting on top of the letter that looked like a street light?
Monkey. That letter makes the same sound as the letter 'M.'

Q28. Which animal was balancing on the spinning dot of the letter that looks like a pot?
Narwhal. This Dot -on- a- pot letter makes the same sound as the letter 'N.'

Q29. Which animal was playing the ring toss game with the letter that looks like a ring?
Hippo. The letter that looks like a ring makes the 'HAA' sound.

Q30. What do you say when you see a bendy glow stick? Which animal was taking guest names for glow-in-the-dark party?
You say, 'Oh WOW!!". Walrus. The bendy glowstick makes the same sound as of letter 'W.'

Q31. What do you say when you see a swan letter on two eggs? Which animal came to see this letter?
You say, 'Oh YAA!'. Unicorns. This letter makes the same sound as the long U or 'Y' sound.

Answer key (2)

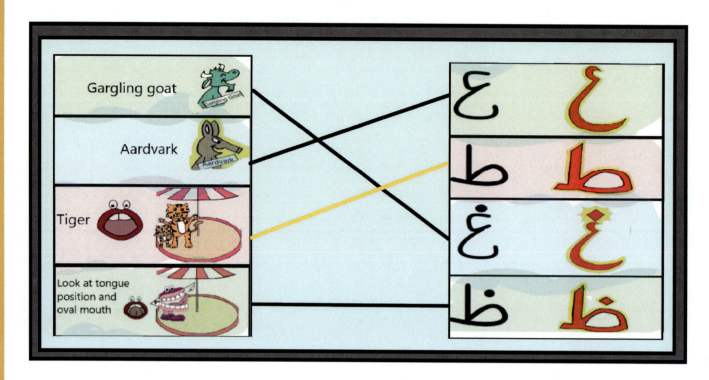

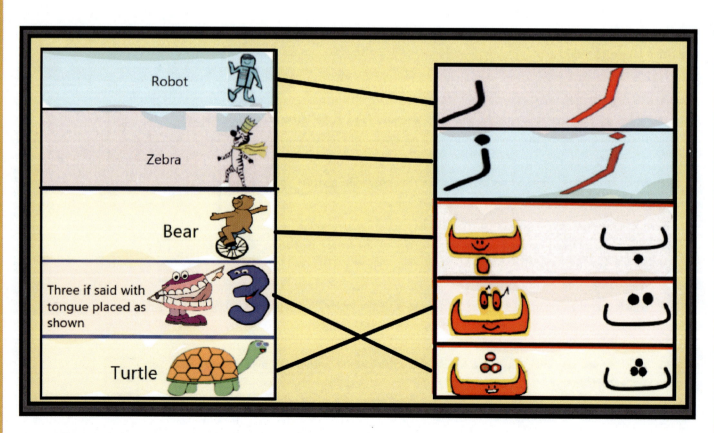

Answer Key (3)

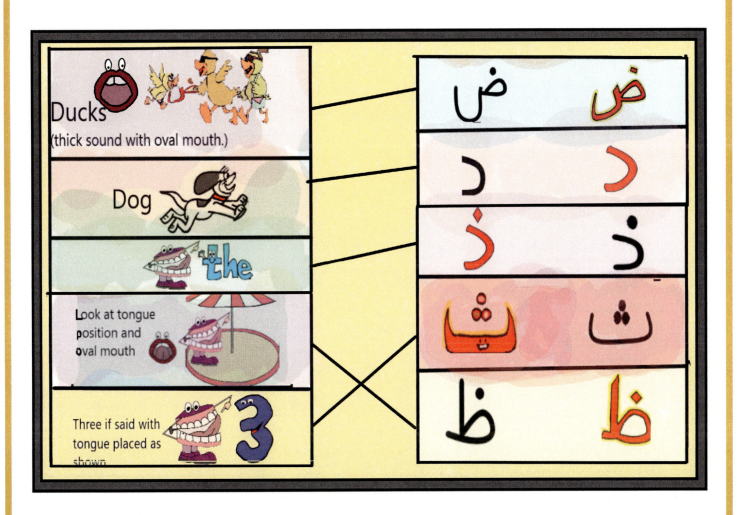

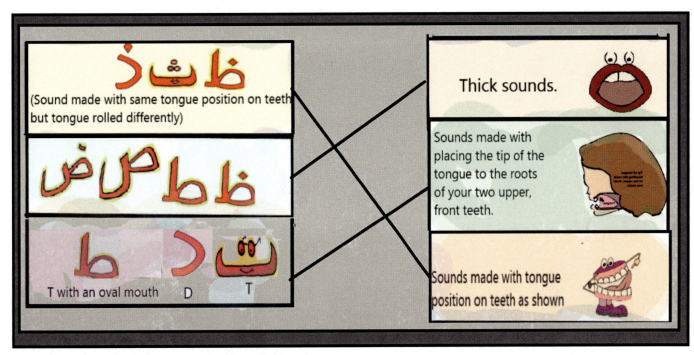

Answer key(4)

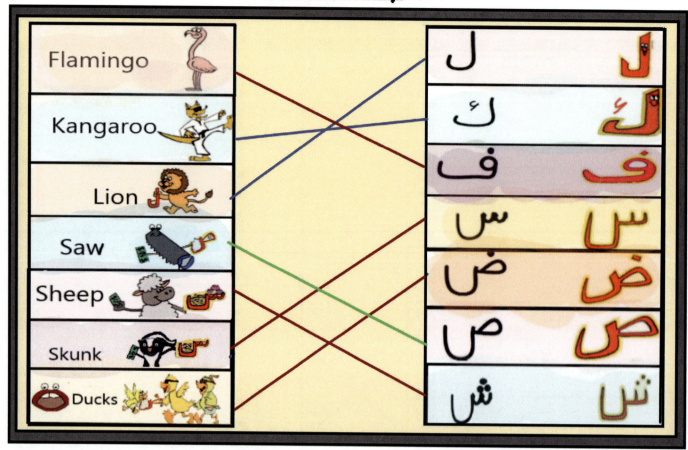

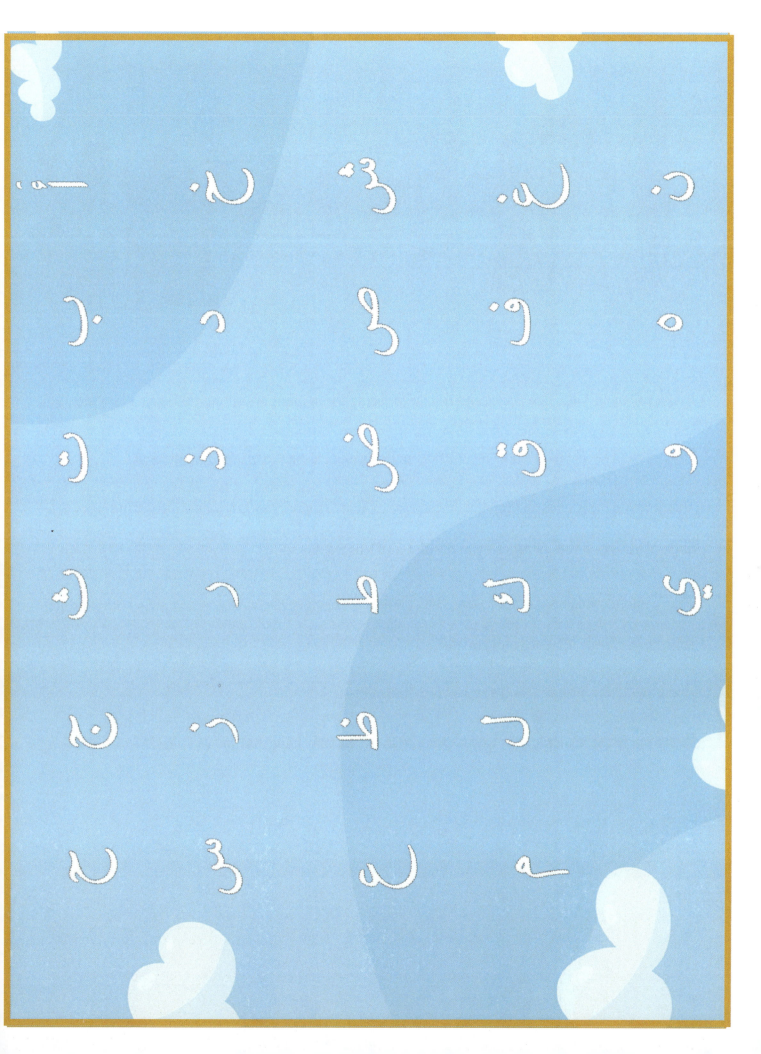

Thank you to my kids Aiza, Aariz, and Amaar for being the inspiration behind this book. I love you guys.

Thank you to Dr. Aysha Wazwaz for overseeing the pronunciation guide used in this book.

Thank you to my friends and family who generously contributed to my fundraiser for getting this book illustrated. Thank you for believing in my idea and trusting me.

Thank you Maira Jamil, Ayesha R., and Patty Stadem for being my beta readers and giving me glowing reviews. I am truly humbled and grateful.

Thank you to my husband for his support in this process.

Thank you to the reader for giving my book a chance. I humbly hope that you will like it.

Note to the teachers/parents/caregivers

To reinforce letter-sound association, read the book with the child, then:

1. Turn to the Arabic letters chart.

2. Point to a letter and ask what fair attraction it reminds the child of from the book. Offer prompts if needed.

3. Ask which animal/character was interacting with this letter in the book. Offer prompts if needed.

4. Based on the name of the animal/character and the summary boxes, help them figure out what sound the letter makes.

5. Review the letter's page, observing details to create a positive association.

Repeat steps 1-5 as desired, possibly after re-reading the book.

Prompt options for letter shape resemblance:

1.	Pole	7.	Teacups	13.	Ladle
2.	Canoes	8.	Merry-go-round ride	14.	Streetlight
3.	Roller coasters	9.	Sky ride	15.	Game bowl (spinning dot)
4.	Boomerangs	10.	Boat ride with a shelf	16.	Ring
5.	Slides	11.	Game bowl (two eyes and open mouth)	17.	Bendy glowstick
6.	Food bowls	12.	Bumper car	18.	Celebrity swan (on two eggs)

Example of an Arabic letter whose sound exists in English:	Example of an Arabic letter whose sound doesn't exist in English:
1. What does this letter shape remind you of from the story? A food bowl, canoe, or slide?	What does this letter shape remind you of from the story? A food bowl, canoe, or slide?
2. There were two slide letters; one with a dot and the other without. Which slide is this?	There were three canoe letters. Was this canoe doing a rope balancing act, a fun glasses party, or a three-scoops ice cream party?
3. Identify the correct characters/animals waiting to ride the slide with no dot (raccoon, rabbit, rhino, robot).	What characters/animals were getting ice cream or hanging out with this letter? (number three and the teeth character).
4. Check the summary box for the letter's sound and ask the child what sound it makes based on the character names. The correct answer is 'R.'	The summary box confirms that the letter's sound doesn't exist in English. Ask the child what sound it makes based on the two characters. The correct answer is the sound made when saying 'three' with tongue placement shown by the teeth character. Play an audio recording if needed.

Made in the USA
Las Vegas, NV
19 March 2024